Wonders of the World

DATE DUE

Serie   r

Pearson Education Limited

Edinburgh Gate, Harlow,
Essex CM20 2JE, England
and Associated Companies throughout the world.

ISBN: 978-1-4082-3200-2

This edition first published by Pearson Education Ltd 2010

7 9 10 8

Text copyright © Vicky Shipton 2010

Illustrations by Oxford Designers & Illustrators

The moral rights of the authors have been asserted in accordance with
the Copyright Designs and Patents Act 1988

Set in 12/15.5pt A. Garamond
Printed in China
SWTC/07

Penguin Books Ltd a Penguin Random House company

Acknowledgements

(Key: b-bottom; c-centre; l-left; r-right; t-top)

4Corners Images: SIME / Guido Baviera 18; Guido Cozzi 16, 20l; Paul Panayiotou 2, 8bc, 43r, 44; SIME / Bruno Cossa 7t; 8tc; SIME / Bruno Morandi 25tr; SIME / Giovanni Simeone 28, 43l; SIME / Ingrid Siewert 33 (D), 36b; SIME / Johanna Huber 33 (E), 38; SIME / Laurent Grandadam 5t, 8br, 43c; SIME / Olimpio Fantuz 25bl; SIME / Otto Stadler 3, 8tl; **Alamy Images:** Roberta Allen 27b; Chad Ehlers 33 (B), 39; Russell Kord 23b; Art Kowalsky 11; David Muenker 33 (C), 34-35, 36t; Pictorial Press Ltd 27t; PjrFoto / Phil Robinson 1; Rob Walls 31b; Peter M. Wilson 23t; **Corbis:** amanaimages / Yoshitsugu Nishigaki 10; Atlantide Phototravel 7b, 8bl; Lloyd Cluff 12; David Kadlubowski 35r; Rudy Sulgan 29; Jim Zuckerman / © ADAGP, Paris and DACS, London 2009 17br; **Foster + Partners:** Architects of Crystal Island 31t; **Getty Images:** AFP 5b; AFP / Hiro Yamagata 37; David Sanger 30; Travel Ink 33 (A); Nevada Wier 13; **iStockphoto:** Kjell Brynildsen 17cl, 20r; Izabela Habur 22; Holger Mette 6t, 8tr; **Photolibrary.com:** Photographer's Choice RF 24; **Photoshot Holdings Limited:** World Pictures 19b; WpN 19t; **SuperStock:** Hidekazu Nishibata 17tr, 20c

All other images © Pearson Education

Picture research by Frances Topp

Every effort has been made to trace the copyright holders and we apologise in
advance for any unintentional omissions. We would be pleased to insert the
appropriate acknowledgement in any subsequent edition of this publication.

For a complete list of the titles available in the Penguin Active Reading series please write to your local
Pearson Longman office or to: Penguin Readers Marketing Department, Pearson Education,
Edinburgh Gate, Harlow, Essex CM20 2JE, England.

Contents

	Activities 1	iv
Chapter 1	Ancient Wonders	1
	Activities 2	8
Chapter 2	Bridges, Dams, and Canals	10
	Activities 3	14
Chapter 3	Statues and Islands	16
	Activities 4	20
Chapter 4	Works of Rulers and Religion	22
	Activities 5	26
Chapter 5	Bigger and Taller!	28
	Activities 6	32
Chapter 6	Natural Wonders	34
	Talk about it	40
	Write about it	41
	Project: Wonder Vacations	42

1.1 What's the book about?

Look at the pictures and talk to another student.

1 Can you find all of these in your country? Name some of them.

2 Which are the most famous in the world?

canals: the Panama Canal, the Suez Canal ...

1.2 What comes first?

Look at the pictures in Chapter 1. What do you know about these old places? Which countries are they in? What were they for? Make notes in your notebook.

The Great Pyramid (page 2)   Chichen Itza (page 3)

The Great Wall of China (pages 4–5)   Petra (page 6)

The Colosseum (page 7)   Machu Picchu (page 7).

Ancient Wonders

How can we say that one building is more "important" than another from a different time and place?

In **Ancient** Greece, about 2,500 years **ago**, the writer Herodotus made a famous **list** of seven great places. Five of these places were Greek. (Herodotus was Greek!) But Herodotus called his list the "Seven **Wonders** of the World." Many people at that time wanted to see the famous places on the list.

Today only one thing on Herodotus's list is standing—the Great Pyramid in Egypt—but many people today discuss the "wonders of the world." Often they list only seven new wonders because there were seven things on the first list. But of course there are many important, interesting, and beautiful places in the world. So which seven places go on the list? This is a very difficult question. Do buildings go on the list because they are the biggest—or the most important? And how can we say that one building is more "important" than another from a different time and place?

Some of the wonders of the world are old and some are new. Some are buildings and some are **natural** wonders. In this book, you can read about all kinds of wonderful places.

ancient /ˈeɪnʃənt/ (Adj) An *ancient* building is very, very old.
ago /əˈɡoʊ/ (adv) Herodotus lived a long time *ago*.
list /lɪst/ (n/v) Before they go to a supermarket, many people write a *list*. They only buy things from their list.
wonder /ˈwʌndə/ (n) A *wonder* is a great or beautiful thing.
natural /ˈnætʃərəl/ (adj) Trees, rivers, and mountains are all *natural* things.

Pyramids

Some of the most famous—and the strangest—ancient buildings are pyramids.

The Great Pyramid

The Great Pyramid at Giza, near Cairo in Egypt, was on Herodotus's list of Seven Wonders, and it is very famous today, too. This pyramid is 4,500 years old and 150 meters tall. People think that there are about 2.3 **million** big **stones** in it. Each stone is very heavy—more than 2,000 kilos. So how did the Egyptians build the pyramid with these big, heavy stones? There are a lot of ideas, but we do not really know.

We do know the answer to another question—*why* did the Egyptians build the pyramids? For the ancient Egyptians, the end of life in our world was the start of another life. The pyramids were for the country's dead **rulers**. The dead rulers—and many of their things—went into the pyramid. The rulers were rich when they were dead, too!

Khufu built the Great Pyramid. It took about twenty years. Inside the pyramid there are three big rooms.

Today Giza is one of the most famous places in the world. The Great Pyramid and the other two pyramids there are a bridge to the ancient world.

million /ˈmɪlyən/ (n) One *million* is 1,000,000.
stone /stoʊn/ (n) *Stone* is very hard ground. We often build walls with *stone*.
ruler /ˈrulə/ (n) The *ruler* is the head of a country.

Chichen Itza

The Egyptian pyramids are not the only pyramids in the world. You can also see pyramids in **parts** of Mexico.

Chichen Itza was an important city of the Mayan people in the Yucatan **area** of Mexico. The Mayans started to build it in the sixth **century**, but the city was at its biggest and most important hundreds of years later. At one time there were hundreds of buildings in the city.

Now visitors can see about thirty buildings. The biggest is the Temple of Kukulkan in the center of the city. Inside the pyramid there is a second, older temple with stairs down to a room with a ruler's chair and a statue.

Near the pyramid is a big place for a Mayan ball game. How dangerous was this game? A picture in stone on one of the walls gives the answer. It shows some ball players, and one of them has no head!

part /pɑrt/ (n) A *part* is some, but not all of something.
area /ˈɛriə/ (n) An *area* is a big part of a country.
century /ˈsɛntʃəri/ (n) A *century* is 100 years.

3

The Great Wall of China

Which is the most famous wall in the world? For many people, there is only one answer to this question— the Great Wall of China. Its name in Chinese means "long wall." This is a good name because at one time the wall was about 6,400 kilometers long.

The Chinese first built a long wall about 2,500 years ago (at about the time of Herodotus in Greece). It **protected** the country in the north. They built a second wall—today's Great Wall of China—about five hundred years ago. It was more than a wall; they put towers in high places on it. At one time more than one million men worked on the wall and protected their country.

Today many people visit the Great Wall every year. Some parts are more famous than other parts. Visitors often go to a part of the wall to the north of the city of Beijing. One place here is 7.8 meters high and 5 meters wide. Some of the most famous and beautiful parts of the wall climb through the mountains. The highest tower is at 980 meters.

Of course, some parts of the wall are not there now. In some places, a long way from cities, people used the stones for other buildings. In one place wind and rain are making the wall smaller and smaller. Years ago the wall was 5 meters high there; now it is only about 2 meters.

---

protect /prəˈtɛkt/ (v) Parents *protect* their children from dangerous things. A building can give *protection* from very bad weather.

From the Moon?

Can a person see the Great Wall of China from the **moon**? Many people think that you can. But Neil Armstrong, the first man on the moon, says that it is not possible.

There *is* a photo of the wall from about 160 kilometers up. But from here you can see other buildings, too.

moon /mun/ (n) The *moon* goes around our world every month.

5

Around the Ancient World

Today it is not possible to visit six of the seven ancient wonders on Herodotus's list. But you can see other great, old places around the world.

Petra

Many movie lovers know the ancient city of Petra, in Jordan, because one of its temples is in the third Indiana Jones movie. The city of Petra is more than 2,500 years old. The people of Petra cut many of the city's buildings into the red **rock** of the mountains in the area. Petra was an important center in the area for centuries. But the city's best years were almost at an end when the Romans arrived in the area. For centuries nobody lived there and nobody outside the area knew about the city.

The Colosseum

People liked sports in Ancient Rome, and the Colosseum was an important place for them. But these games were very different from sports today. At one time, 50,000 Romans sat in the Colosseum in Rome and watched fight after fight. Sometimes men fought men; sometimes they fought wild animals. (The Romans brought animals from Africa to Rome for the games.) When the Colosseum opened, 11,000 animals died in the first hundred days.

rock /rɑk/ (n) When you *cut* into a mountain, you find rock.

Machu Picchu

Like Petra, nobody knew about Machu Picchu for a long time. The Inca people built this city high in the mountains of Peru, 80 kilometers from the city of Cuzco, in about 1460. Why did they build a city up there? Some people think that it was for the protection of the Inca people. Other people say that Inca rulers in Cuzco enjoyed summers there. Today visitors to the city can take a train from Cuzco, or they can walk there. This can take about a week!

The world is full of beautiful and interesting ancient buildings and places. You can visit the Parthenon in Athens, Stonehenge in Britain, the Old City of Jerusalem . . . But more and more visitors are going to these ancient places, so we have to protect these wonders carefully.

2.1 Were you right?

Look at your answers to Activity 1.2 on page iv. Then write the name and the country below each picture.

....

....

....

....

....

....

....

....

....

....

....

....

2.2 What more did you learn?

Are the sentences right (✓) or wrong (✗)?

1 The writer Herodotus made a famous list of eight places.

2 All of the places from Herodotus's list are standing now.

3 There are two smaller pyramids next to the Great Pyramid.

4 The pyramid at Chichen Itza is older than the Great Pyramid at Giza.

5 In Chinese the name of the Great Wall means "many stones."

6 You cannot see the Great Wall of China from the moon.

7 People brought red rocks to Petra from a long way away.

8 Sometimes men fought wild animals in the Colosseum.

9 The city of Cuzco is high in the mountains above Machu Picchu.

2.3 Language in use

Read the sentences on the right. Then finish the sentences below with *but* or *so*.

Today only one thing on Herodotus's list is standing, **but** many people today discuss the "wonders of the world."

More and more visitors are going to these ancient places, **so** we have to protect these wonders carefully.

1 There are many important, interesting places in the world, …….. there are many different lists of "wonders."

2 There are about twenty-three million heavy stones in the pyramid, …….. a lot of people worked very hard.

3 The Great Pyramid is the most famous pyramid in the world, …….. it is not the only pyramid.

4 There is a picture of one ball player with no head, …….. the game was dangerous!

5 The Great Wall is very big, …….. you cannot see it from the moon.

6 Petra was an important center, …….. its best years ended a long time ago.

7 Summers in Peru are hot, …….. the Incas built Machu Picchu in the mountains.

2.4 What's next?

Make lists of famous bridges, dams, and canals.

Bridges

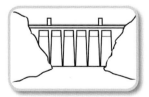

Dams

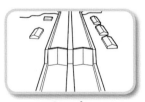

Canals

……………………………… ……………………………… ………………………………

……………………………… ……………………………… ………………………………

……………………………… ……………………………… ………………………………

……………………………… ……………………………… ………………………………

CHAPTER 2

Bridges, Dams, and Canals

In the world today, bridge-builders can build bigger and longer bridges. And they are doing it!

Most of our world is water, so of course water is an important part of many of the world's wonders.

Bridges

Why are some bridges famous? Every day visitors walk across the beautiful Rialto Bridge in Venice. Maybe people know London Bridge from the children's song "London Bridge is falling down." The Golden Gate Bridge in San Francisco is not the longest bridge in the world now, but many people know the famous red bridge. Today other bridges around the world are longer and taller.

The Akashi-Kaikyo Bridge

This bridge goes from the Japanese city of Kobe to Awaji Island— almost 4,000 meters. There are almost 2,000 meters between the bridge's two towers—the longest part of this kind of bridge in the world in 2008. The bridge is very tall because ships have to go under it.

Ten million people worked on the bridge for ten years, and it opened in 1998. The weather in this area is sometimes very bad. The Akashi-Kaikyo can stand in winds of 290 kilometers an hour without a problem.

The Millau Bridge

Drivers between Paris and Spain know the Millau Bridge in the south of France well. This bridge goes high over the River Tarn in France's beautiful Languedoc area.

Work started in 2001, and was fast. The bridge opened at the end of 2004. It's 2,460 meters long and it has seven towers. The top of the towers is 343 meters high—that is taller than the Eiffel Tower! On one part of the bridge, cars are 270 meters above the river. Drivers often stop and take photos.

◆

In the world today, bridge-builders can build bigger and longer bridges. And they are doing it! Builders are working on the Sundra Strait Bridge in Indonesia. There will be 3,000 meters between its towers and the bridge will be 26 kilometers long.

Dams

Rivers bring water, and water brings life to an area. But sometimes there is no water at the right time. One answer to this problem is a dam.

The Aswan High Dam

In Egypt, there is not much water, so the River Nile is very important. In 1960, Nasser began work on an important new plan for his country. Egyptian workers started to build a new dam across the River Nile. Many people had to leave their homes for this. The work finished in 1972, two years after Nasser died.

Now there is a lot of water from the Nile in a new lake, Lake Nasser, behind the Aswan High Dam (121 meters tall and 20 kilometers wide). This lake is almost 500 kilometers long and more than 20 kilometers wide. In years without a lot of rain, Egyptians use water from Lake Nasser. The dam also makes a lot of the country's **electricity**.

Other Dams

Some other famous dams are:

• the Hoover Dam: Seventy years ago, this dam between Arizona and Nevada in the United States was the biggest in the world. Water from the Colorado River goes into Lake Mead behind this dam.

• the Itaipu Dam: This big dam, on the Parana River between Brazil and Paraguay, makes most of Paraguay's electricity. The word *Itaipu* means "sound of the stone."

electricity /ɪˌlɛkˈtrɪsəṭ i,i-/ (n) Televisions and most lights have to have *electricity*.

• the Three Gorges Dam: This new dam, on China's Yangtse River, is bigger than the Itaipu.

• North Sea Protection Works: This dam protects the Netherlands from the waters of the North Sea.

Canals

Sometimes people want a river in a new, different place. What can they do? They can make an **artificial** river—a canal.

The Panama Canal

Vasco Nunez de Balboa first had the idea for a Panama canal about five hundred years ago because this part of Central America, with the Pacific to the west and the Atlantic to the east, is not very wide. Why not build a canal between the two?

It was a good idea, but a difficult job. It was not possible for hundreds of years. North American workers started to build the canal in 1904. They finished the 80-kilometer canal ten years later. Today, the Panama Canal is very important for the world's ships. They do not have to go down and around the bottom of South America.

artificial /ˌɑrʧəˈfɪʃəl/ (adj) An *artificial* thing is not natural.

13

3.1 Were you right?

Look at your answers to Activity 2.4.

1 Which bridges, dams, and canals on your list were in Chapter 2?

2 Why did people build them? What do you remember about them from your reading? Talk about these questions with other students.

3.2 What more did you learn?

1 Put the bridges in the right order from the shortest (1) to the longest (3).

a The Sundra Strait Bridge $\bigcirc$

b The Akashi-Kaikyo Bridge $\bigcirc$

c The Millau Bridge $\bigcirc$

2 Match each dam with its river.

a The Aswan High Dam Parana River

b The Hoover Dam Yangtze River

c The Three Gorges Dam Colorado River

d The Itaipu Dam River Nile

3 Finish these sentences. Write one word in each place.

The Panama Canal is about ª....................... hundred years old. It runs between the ᵇ....................... Ocean and the ᶜ....................... Ocean. Before the canal, ships had to go around the bottom of ᵈ....................... America. Now, they can go across ᵉ....................... America, so many trips are quicker.

.3 Language in use

Read the sentences on the right. Then answer the questions below.

> Today other bridges around the world are **longer** and **taller**.
>
> That is **taller than** the Eiffel Tower!

Bridge	Opened when?	How long?	How tall?
The Golden Gate Bridge	1937	2,737 meters	227.4 meters
The Akashi-Kaikyo Bridge	1998	3,911 meters	298.3 meters
The Millau Bridge	2004	2,460 meters	343 meters

1 Which is taller, the Golden Gate Bridge or the Millau Bridge?

The Millau Bridge is taller than the Golden Gate Bridge

2 Which is longer, the Akashi-Kaikyo Bridge or the Millau Bridge?

3 Which is shorter, the Golden Gate Bridge or the Akashi-Kaikyo Bridge?

4 Which is newer, the Millau Bridge or the Akashi-Kaikyo Bridge?

5 Which is older, the Millau Bridge or the Golden Gate Bridge?

.4 What's next?

Look at the picture on page 16 of the Easter Island Moai. Which of these sentences are true (T)? What do you think?

1 There are 20 statues on Easter Island.

2 These statues are more than 15 meters tall.

3 They are about 100 years old.

4 The statues were a kind of clock for the people of the island.

5 Most of the statues have their backs to the ocean.

CHAPTER 3

Statues and Islands

Why did the islanders make these big stone statues hundreds of years ago? The people of the island did not write, so we do not know.

Beautiful or interesting statues are wonders of the world to many people, and there are of course beautiful natural islands. But we are also building wonderful *artificial* islands for our use.

Statues

One of Herodotus's ancient Seven Wonders was a statue on the island of Rhodes. The "Colossus of Rhodes" was more than 30 meters tall.

The Colossus of Rhodes fell centuries ago, but today other statues can go on a list of the wonders of the world.

Moai Statues

Almost 900 of these statues stand on Easter Island—Rapa Nui—in the Pacific Ocean. Sometimes people call them "Easter Island Heads," but most of the statues are not only heads. Most are about 4 meters tall and many of them stand with their backs to the sea. Why did the islanders make these big stone statues hundreds of years ago? The people of the island did not write, so we do not know.

The Statue of the Leshan Buddha

The biggest stone Buddha in the world—more than 71 meters tall and about 1,200 years old—stands outside the Chinese city of Leshan. The city's name means "happy mountain," and the Buddha's face is smiling. Three rivers meet at the feet of the big statue.

The Statue of Liberty

The people of France gave the Statue of Liberty to the United States in 1884. It stands now on an island in New York. Frederic-Auguste Bartholdi made the statue. Its face is, people think, his mother's face! The statue is 93 meters tall. There are stairs up to its head, but visitors cannot go up the arm to the highest part.

Christ the Redeemer

From the top of Corcovado Mountain, this 38-meter statue of Jesus Christ looks down on the Brazilian city of Rio de Janeiro and its beautiful white beaches. The makers of the statue, Heitor da Silva Costa and Paul Landowski, finished it in 1931.

Islands

Some wonders of the world are on islands; other wonders *are* islands.

Venice

One of the world's most famous cities is not only on *one* island; it is on about 120 islands. Some people call Venice, in the north-east of Italy, the "City of Water." There are no big streets, but the city has 150 canals. The longest of these—at only 3 kilometers—is the Grand Canal. People can go around the city in their boats or in "boat taxis" and "boat buses." They can walk around the city easily, too: there are 400 bridges.

Artificial Islands

Not all islands are natural. There are more and more artificial islands in the world. Builders in Japan wanted a new airport near the cities of Kobe and Osaka, but there was no good place for an airport. The answer to the problem? They built an artificial island for Kansai Airport near Osaka. Here the airport can be open twenty-four hours a day and nobody has to hear the airplanes near his or her home.

Work on the island started in 1987, and it took three years. There were 10,000 workers and 80 ships. The builders made the island with the stone from three mountains! It is 4 kilometers long and 2.5 kilometers wide. Then, in 1991, the builders started work on the airport building.

There is always one big problem with artificial islands—they slowly go down into the water. This happened with the Kansai island, also—it went down 8 meters in its first years. This problem cost the builders of the island a lot of money.

Palm Islands, Dubai

Dubai has beautiful hot weather for visitors. But people like beaches and Dubai wanted more. The answer was easy—they built islands with more beaches. Work on the three islands started in 2003. They are very different from other natural islands and you can see that from above. There are now homes, apartments, stores, and workplaces on them. More than one million people can live there. Many visitors from around the world come to the islands for vacations.

Next, builders in Dubai built "The World." This has 300 small islands. Again, you can understand the name when you see the islands from above. With these and the three Palm Islands, there are now 1,500 kilometers of new beach in Dubai. And there will be more artificial islands there.

4.1 Were you right?

1 Look at your answers to Activity 3.4. Then write in the chart.

Statues	How tall?	How old?
Moai statues		
The Leshan Buddha		
The Statue of Liberty		
Christ the Redeemer		

2 Match each sentence with a photo. Write the letters, A–C.

1 France gave this to the United States. ◯

2 Three rivers meet at its feet. ◯

3 There are almost 900 of these statues. ◯

4.2 What more did you learn?

Finish the sentences with these words.

> **artificial   beaches   natural   Water   mountains   taxis**

1 Some people call Venice the "City of ...."

2 In Venice people often move around by "boat ...."

3 In Japan they built an .... island for a new airport.

4 They made the island with stone from three ....

5 Dubai now has 1,500 kilometers of new ....

6 The islands in Dubai are different from other .... islands.

3 Language in use

Read the sentences on the right. Then finish the sentences below. Use words from the box and put them in the past tense.

> They **built** an artificial island.
>
> The builders **made** the island with stone.

be   build   can   cost   fall   give

1 We cannot see the "Colossus of Rhodes" today because it .... centuries ago.

2 The people of France .... the Statue of Liberty to the United States.

3 There .... no good place for an airport.

4 This problem .... a lot of money.

5 They .... homes and workplaces on the islands.

6 People .... visit the islands.

4 What's next?

The next chapter tells you about these places:

the Forbidden City   the Alhambra   the Taj Mahal
Hagia Sophia   Angkor Wat   the Leaning Tower of Pisa

Look at the pictures on pages 22–25, then discuss these questions. What do you think?

1 Which building's name means "the red palace?"

2 Which place has a 10-meter wall around its buildings?

3 In which place do visitors first go across a bridge?

4 Which building takes its name from somebody's wife?

5 Which building was a place for Christians and then for Muslims?

6 Which building looks very dangerous?

CHAPTER 4

Works of Rulers and Religion

Many people think that the Taj Mahal, outside Agra in India, is the most beautiful building in the world. It takes its name from a woman.

People built many of the most famous buildings in the world for great rulers or for their churches. They could go into the churches, but usually they could not visit the palaces.

Rulers' Buildings

Countries' rulers often built great buildings. They often lived in them or visited them. They were rich and they wanted to show that to their people and to the world.

The Forbidden City

Between the years 1420 and 1911, the Forbidden City in Beijing was home to twenty-four Chinese rulers. Yong Le built the palace when he made Beijing his most important city. A 10-meter wall runs around the buildings. At one time, 6,000 people could live in the Forbidden City. But people from outside could visit only when the ruler said yes. The Forbidden City was not open to most people.

The Alhambra

The Alhambra stands in Granada, in the south of Spain. Its name comes from the Arabic language and means "the red palace." The Moorish rulers of Granada built the palace between 1238 and 1354.

Centuries later, people used the Alhambra for many different things. At one time it was a home for Napoleon's men from France.

The Taj Mahal

Many people think that the Taj Mahal, outside Agra in India, is the most beautiful building in the world. It takes its name from a woman—one of Shah Jahan's wives. Shah Jahan built the Taj Mahal for her, but it was not a home. He built it when she died in 1632.

Twenty-two thousand people worked on the building for more than twenty years. The outside of the building is white stone, and it looks very different at different times of day. People say that the Taj Mahal is most beautiful by the light of the full moon.

Religious Buildings

Many of the wonders of the world are **religious** buildings. Some of these were important to more than one religion.

Hagia Sophia, Istanbul

Part of Istanbul is in Europe and part of the city is in Asia. Justinian I built one of Istanbul's most important buildings in the sixth century, when the name of the city was Constantinople. First, it was a Christian church. When the Ottomans took the city in 1453, ruler Mehmed II gave the city its new name. The church was at that time a Muslim mosque. It had four new towers. Today followers of Islam, Christianity, and other religions can visit and enjoy this beautiful building.

Angkor Wat

At one time, Angkor in Cambodia was the biggest city in the world. From 802 to 1327, it was the Khmer people's most important city, and the city's biggest building was the temple, Angkor Wat. First, in the twelfth century, it was a Hindu temple.

religious /rɪˈlɪdʒəs/ (adj) A church is a *religious* building. Islam, Christianity, and Hinduism are different kinds of religion.

When the people of the city saw the temple's five towers, they thought about an important mountain for Hindus, Mount Meru. Later, Angkor Wat was a Buddhist temple. Visitors to Angkor Wat have to walk across a 188-meter bridge.

The Leaning Tower of Pisa

"Is it going to fall?" think many visitors to the tower in Pisa. But this famous Italian tower is standing today. It is part of the city's cathedral. The first part of the work on the tower started in 1173. Five years later, the builders saw a big problem—the tower **leaned** to the south. The work stopped. It did not start again for one hundred years. At this time, the Church built more of the tower. The new part leaned to the north. The Church put the third and last part of the tower on top one hundred years after that.

Will the tower fall? Many people are working hard on this problem. They hope that the answer is "No!"

lean /lin/ (v) You can *lean* back in a big chair.

5.1 Were you right?

Look at your answers to Activity 4.4. Then circle the right words for each sentence.

1 There was a wall around the Forbidden City in Beijing because it

was *not open to most people / protected the city*.

2 The name of the Alhambra *is Spanish / comes from Arabic*.

3 Shah Jahan built the Taj Mahal when *one of his wives died /*

he married a new wife.

4 The name of Hagia Sophia's city changed from

Constantinople to Istanbul / Istanbul to Constantinople.

5 When the Khmer people saw Angkor Wat's five towers, they thought of

a famous bridge / an important mountain.

6 Work on the tower in Pisa stopped for one hundred years because

the first part of the tower *fell / leaned*.

5.2 What more did you learn?

Write questions for the answers below.

1 ....

The Moorish rulers of Granada built it.

2 ....

Some people say that it is most beautiful by the light of the full moon.

3 ....

The temple has five towers.

4 ....

The first part of the work started in 1173.

3 Language in use

Read the sentence on the right. Then match the sentence parts below.

> They **could** go into the churches, but usually they **could** not visit the palaces.

1 At one time 6,000 people could ...

2 People from outside could only ...

3 After 1453 Muslims could ...

4 The first builders could not ...

5 In the past many rulers were rich, so they could ...

6 Napoleon's men could ...

a live in the Forbidden City.

b finish the tower in Pisa.

c stay in the Alhambra.

d visit when the ruler said yes.

e build beautiful palaces.

f go into Hagia Sophia.

4 What's next?

Discuss the pictures. What do you think?

1 What can you see in the first picture?

2 What is the name of the building?

3 Which city is this building in?

4 Why did King Kong climb this building?

5 Which tall buildings are important in other movies?

6 What is the name of the tower in the second picture?

7 Which city is it in?

8 How old is it?

9 What is the tallest building in your country? What do people use it for?

10 What is the world's tallest building? What do people use it for?

CHAPTER 5

Bigger and Taller!

*At times it was a race between some of the big cities
for the tallest building in the world.*

Today it is possible to make much bigger and taller buildings than the buildings of centuries ago.

The Race to the Top

In the nineteenth century, buildings changed. People had new ideas, and they knew more about building. So builders could go higher and higher.

The Eiffel Tower

What is the most famous place in Paris? Most people give the same answer—the Eiffel Tower. It was the idea of Gustave Eiffel. (Eiffel also worked on the Statue of Liberty.) Some people in Paris did not like the plans for the tower. But the world was different now. More and more was possible, and Eiffel understood this.

He finished the tower and showed it to the world in 1889. At the time it was the tallest building in the world—324 meters. Eiffel understood one of the biggest problems for tall buildings—the wind. Strong winds are not a problem for the Eiffel Tower because they can go through it.

Visitors loved the tower from the start. In its first year, tickets paid for the tower. The Eiffel Tower is the tallest building in Paris today, but there are many taller buildings around the world. This does not stop the millions of visitors—almost 6.5 million every year.

The Empire State Building

Is the Empire State Building the most famous new building in the world? People in New York think that it is!

William Lamb finished the Empire State Building in 1931. At 443 meters, it was the tallest building in the world, and it stayed the tallest for forty-one years. From the 86th floor and the 102nd floor visitors can look down on New York City. On a good day, you can see almost 130 kilometers from up there. On one day every year there is a big **race** up the stairs to the top. One man ran to the top in about ten minutes.

The Empire State Building is also in a lot of movies. The first film was *King Kong* in 1933. At the end of the film, King Kong climbs to the top of the building (with a woman in his hand!) and fights airplanes.

The race continues

After the 1970s, there were more and more very tall buildings. At times it was a race between some of the big cities for the tallest building in the world.

race /reɪs/ (n) The shortest *race* in the Olympic Games is the 100 meters.

This race brought some interesting questions:

• How is a "tower" different from a "building"? People can go to the top of a "tower." But they do not usually live or work in it. This language problem is worse because some buildings have the word "tower" in their name. The CN Tower in Toronto is really a tower, but the Petronas Towers in Kuala Lumpur are buildings!

• What is really the top of a building? Is it the highest thing on the building or does it have to be part of the building? People have different ideas about this. Most people say that the Petronas Towers (1998) are taller than the Sears Tower (1973) in Chicago because their highest part is part of the building.

In the same way, most people say that Taipei 101 (2004) is taller than the Shanghai World Financial Center (2008). But the Shanghai World Financial Center has a higher floor with people on it.

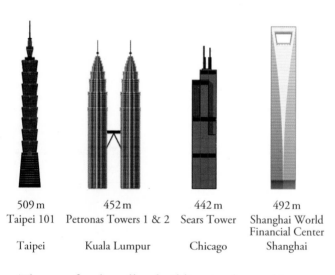

509 m	452 m	442 m	492 m
Taipei 101	Petronas Towers 1 & 2	Sears Tower	Shanghai World Financial Center
Taipei	Kuala Lumpur	Chicago	Shanghai

The race for the tallest building in the world never stops. The new winner of the race is the Burj Dubai. Before work ended, it was the tallest building in the world at 818 meters.

Bigger and Bigger

Some new buildings are not high, but they are big—very big. But the biggest buildings are not always the most interesting. A building at Beijing airport is one of the biggest in the world, but most visitors are more interested in the Forbidden City.

Crystal Island

What next? In Moscow, builders are working on Crystal Island. At 450 meters tall, it will not be one of the world's tallest buildings, but it will be very, very big It will have 900 apartments, 3,000 hotel rooms, a school for 500 children, movie theaters, places for sports, and more. The builder calls it "a city in a building."

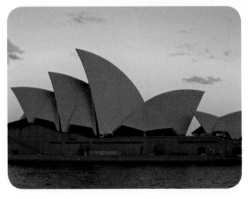

Of course, there are smaller new buildings on most lists of world wonders. One famous twentieth century building is the Sydney **Opera** House in Australia. Many people see the top of the white building and think of ships.

opera /ˈɑprə, ˈɑpərə/ (n) *Opera* lovers watch singers in a theater.

6.1 Were you right?

Look at your answers to Activity 5.4. Then read these sentences and write the names of the buildings.

1 It is the tallest building in Paris today.

....

2 Every year there is a race up the stairs to the top.

....

3 It was in the King Kong movies.

....

4 This is the biggest building in the world, not the tallest.

....

5 Its builders call it "a city in a building."

....

6 People listen to music here.

....

6.2 What more did you learn?

These sentences are wrong. Change them and make them right.

1 Nineteenth-century visitors did not like the Eiffel Tower.

....

2 The Empire State Building was the tallest building in the world for almost forty years.

....

3 Most people think that the Petronas Towers are not as tall as the Sears Tower.

....

4 Most visitors to Beijing are more interested in the big airport building than the Forbidden City.

....

5 People see the top of the Sydney Opera House and think of mountains.

....

6 Builders are working on Crystal Island in Dubai.

....

5.3 Language in use

Read the sentences on the right. Then finish the sentences below. Use the words in the box and write about the future.

> Crystal Island **will be** bigger than the Beijing Airport. It **will have** 900 apartments.

be go live build stop play visit watch

1 People ...will live....... in the Crystal Island's 900 apartments.

2 There .... 3,000 hotel rooms.

3 People .... sports there.

4 People .... movies in the movie theaters.

5 500 children .... to school inside the building.

6 What .... builders .... next?

7 The race for the tallest and biggest building .... not ....

8 But next year 6.5 million people .... the Eiffel Tower.

5.4 What's next?

Match the sentences with the pictures (A–E).

1 Climbers call it "the top of the world."

2 It is very important to Aborigines.

3 It takes its name from a British ruler.

4 A big river runs through the red rock.

5 This wonder is not always in the same place.

Mount Everest

the Northern Lights

the Grand Canyon

Victoria Falls

Uluru

33

CHAPTER 6

Natural Wonders

Climbers call the top of Everest "the top of the world." They are usually only "on top of the world" for about half an hour.

Many people think that the best wonders of the world are not the work of men and women. They think that the most beautiful places in the world are the natural wonders.

Canyons

The Grand Canyon is the greatest natural wonder in the United States. Most of the rock is red, but there are lines of rock of different colors—brown, green, and blue.

The Grand Canyon is:
- 446 kilometers long
- between 0.5 and 29 kilometers wide
- 1.6 kilometers from top to bottom at the lowest place.

The Colorado River made the canyon. This river is fast and the rock is not very hard. We know that Native Americans* lived around it 4,000 years ago. Europeans first saw the Grand Canyon in 1540, when Garcia Lopez de Cardenas followed the Colorado River. But Europeans did not go back for 200 years.

Most visitors to the Grand Canyon go to the south part. Here you can walk down to the river at the bottom. You can go down and up again in one day, but this is not a good idea. It is hotter at the bottom, and the climb to the top is very hard. Most people stay at the bottom for a night, and then climb up again the next day. Or you can fly over the Grand Canyon in a small airplane.

In one part of the Grand Canyon you can walk out on to a glass area and look down.

*Native Americans: Native Americans were the first people in America. They lived there before Europeans arrived.

Waterfalls

There are many beautiful and famous waterfalls around the world. Here are three of the most famous:

• Iguazu Falls, on a river between Argentina and Brazil, is one of the greatest places in South America. It is 4 kilometers wide. More than 270 different smaller waterfalls make Iguazu Falls.

• Angel Falls in Venezuela is the highest waterfall in the world—979 meters. (That is twenty times taller than Niagara Falls!) People cannot easily visit Angel Falls on foot. For many years people did not know about the place. Then, in 1935, somebody saw the waterfall from an airplane.

• Victoria Falls is in Africa, between Zimbabwe and Zambia. It has four different waterfalls. A European saw these for the first time in 1855 and he gave them their name. Victoria was the British ruler at that time.

Mountains

Which mountain goes on most lists of natural wonders?
- Mount Fuji? On a good day, you can see Mount Fuji from Tokyo.
- Mount Kilimanjaro? This mountain in Tanzania is the highest place in all of Africa, and there is always snow on the top.
- The Matterhorn? This beautiful mountain is not as tall as some other mountains in the European Alps, but it is very different from other mountains.

But the most famous mountain in the world is also the tallest—Mount Everest. This mountain in the Himalayas is 8,848 meters high.

Many people tried to climb Everest, but it is a dangerous mountain. Sir Edmund Hillary and Tenzing Norgay were the first to the top, in 1953. After them, about 2,500 climbers also arrived at the top. (Almost two hundred other climbers tried and died on the climb.) Climbers call the top of Everest "the top of the world." They are usually only "on top of the world" for about half an hour. Then they have to climb down before it gets dark.

Rocks

Uluru—Ayers Rock—is the most famous natural place in Australia. It is 348 meters high, 3 kilometers from east to west, and 2 kilometers from north to south.

We can only see a small part of it. Most of the rock is under the ground. It is usually red, but it can be different colors at different times of day and in different kinds of weather. A walk around the bottom of Uluru is more than 8 kilometers. Many visitors also climb up to the top, but this can be dangerous.

Uluru is very important for the Aborigine* peoples in the area. Because of this, they do not climb Uluru. It has an important place in their stories about the early days of the world. Inside some parts of Uluru there are Aborigine pictures.

*Aborigine: The Aborigines were the first people in Australia. They were there a long time before Europeans arrived.

Wonders in the Night

Visitors to the north of Scandinavia can see the Aurora Borealis, the Northern Lights. You can see the lights in the north of Alaska, Canada, and Russia, too, but sometimes you have to wait a long time for them!

The night sky is full of beautiful lines of color—usually green and red, sometimes blue. The light is as strong as a full moon sometimes. But not every visitor sees the Northern Lights. They are not always there in the sky. When they are there, they are not always in the same place. One old story in Norway says that the Aurora is a woman in the sky. When she is angry with you, you do not see her.

◆

What is your list of the Seven Wonders of the World? Are your wonders old or new, natural or artificial? Are any of them in your country? Are they all in the pages of this book?

Herodotus only had seven wonders on his list. Maybe people were unhappy about that, too. The number is not important. Our world is full of wonders. Enjoy them!

Talk about it

1 **Work with another student. Discuss these questions. Then discuss the same questions with the class.**

1 You can go and see only one of the places in this book.

    a Which place would you really like to visit? Why?

    b How can you get there? Will the trip be expensive?

    c What other things will you see and do in that country?

    d What will you eat and drink?

    e What will you take with you on the trip?

2 There are many other important "wonders of the world."

    a What are they?

    b Where are they?

    c Why are they more important than the wonders in this book?

    d Why are they not in this book, do you think?

3 Maybe you think that some places in this book are not really "wonders."

    a What are they?

    b Why are they not really important?

4 Think about the protection of ancient wonders.

    a How can we protect them?

    b Why is this sometimes difficult?

2 **Work in three groups. Make notes, then discuss your ideas. Which group has the best ideas?**

| **Group A:** | You think that ancient buildings are the most interesting and beautiful wonders of the world. |

| **Group B:** | You think that new buildings are the most important. |

| **Group C:** | You think that natural places are the true wonders of the world. |

Which building or place from your country do you want to put on a new list of the Seven Wonders of the World? Why? Make notes here. Then write your ideas for the website below.

Notes

Seven Wonders!

In Ancient Greece Herodotus made a list of Seven Wonders of the World. But we can only see one of these wonders today. Send us your ideas for a new list!

Your wonder:

Place and country:

Why is it great?

SEND

1 Work with one or two other students. Your company sells vacations around the world. Now you want to sell vacations to the greatest wonders of the world.

a Write a long list of possible places—from this book, and your ideas. Write them below.

b Give your list to other students. Which would they like to visit? Each person will check (✓) the seven best wonders (the most important, interesting, or beautiful places) on your list.

Great Pyramid
Stonehenge

2 And the winner is . . .!

Look at other students' answers on your list. Write the winners below.

Best new wonder:

Best ancient wonder:

Best island:

Best statue:

Best tower:

Best natural wonder:

3 Discuss the answers to Activities 1 and 2 with your friends. Then list the Seven Wonders of the World for your vacation.

Seven Wonders

1 ....   4 ....

2 ....   5 ....

3 ....   6 ....

                                                    7 ....

4 Read this magazine advertisement, and then write one for your company's new "Wonder Vacations."

Do you want to see the most important and beautiful places in the world?

Go with **Wonder Vacations!**

Visit www.WonderVacations.com and learn more.

5 Write a leaflet for each of the places on your new list.

    a Use this book and other books. Learn more about each place.

    b Why is it a wonder of the world? Tell your customers about it. Write three
       of your leaflets here.

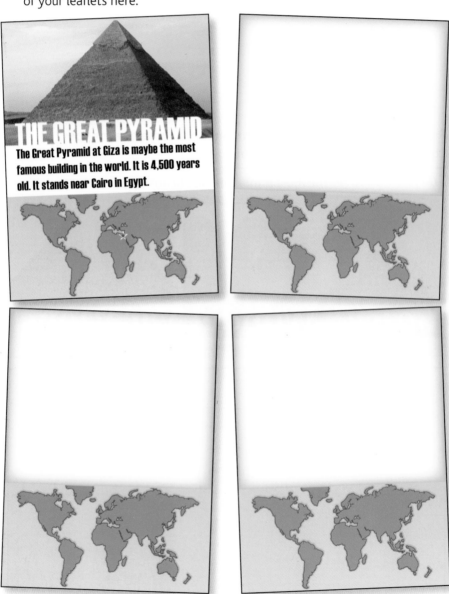

THE GREAT PYRAMID

The Great Pyramid at Giza is maybe the most famous building in the world. It is 4,500 years old. It stands near Cairo in Egypt.